Memories of a Lifetime™

Lace Images

ARTWORK FOR SCRAPBOOKS & FABRIC-TRANSFER CRAFTS

Andrea Vetten-Marley

A LARK/CHAPELLE BOOK
A Division of Sterling Publishing Co., Inc.
New York

A Lark/Chapelle Book

Author: Andrea Vetten-Marley

Chapelle, Ltd., Inc.
P.O. Box 9255, Ogden, UT 84409
(801) 621-2777 • (801) 621-2788 Fax
e-mail: chapelle@chapelleltd.com
Web site: www.chapelleltd.com

10 9 8 7 6 5 4 3 2 1

First Edition

Published by Lark Books, A Division of
Sterling Publishing Co., Inc.
387 Park Avenue South, New York, N.Y. 10016

Distributed in Canada by Sterling Publishing, c/o Canadian Manda Group,
165 Dufferin Street, Toronto, Ontario, Canada M6K 3H6

Distributed in the United Kingdom by GMC Distribution Services,
Castle Place, 166 High Street, Lewes, East Sussex, England BN7 1XU

Distributed in Australia by Capricorn Link (Australia) Pty Ltd.,
P.O. Box 704, Windsor, NSW 2756 Australia

PC Configuration: Windows 98 or later with 128 MB RAM or greater. At least 100 MB
of free hard-disk space. Dual speed or faster CD-ROM drive, and a 24-bit color monitor.

Macintosh Configuration: Mac OS 9 or later with 128 MB RAM or greater. At least
100 MB of free hard-disk space. Dual speed or faster CD-ROM drive, and a 24-bit
color monitor.

Manufactured in China

ISBN 13: 978-1-57990-983-3
ISBN 10: 1-57990-983-3

For information about custom editions, special sales, premium and corporate
purchases, please contact Sterling Special Sales Department at 800-805-5489 or
specialsales@sterlingpub.com.

InTroducTion

Imagine having hundreds of rare vintage images right at your fingertips. With our *Memories of a Lifetime*™ series, that's exactly what you get. We've scoured antique stores, estate sales, and other outlets to find one-of-a-kind images to give your projects the flair that only old-time artwork can provide. From Victorian postcards to hand-painted beautiful borders and frames, it would take years to acquire a collection like this. However, with this easy-to-use resource, you'll have them all—right here, right now.

Each image has been reproduced to the highest quality standard for photocopying and scanning; reduce or enlarge them to suit your needs. A CD-ROM containing all of the images in digital form is included, enabling you to use them for any computer project over and over again. If you prefer to use them as they're printed, simply cut them out—they're printed on one side only.

Perfect for paper crafting, scrapbooking, and fabric transfers, *Memories of a Lifetime* books will inspire you to explore new avenues of creativity. We've included a sampling of ideas to get you started, but the best part is using your imagination to create your own fabulous projects. Be sure to look for other books in this series as we continue to search the markets for wonderful vintage images.

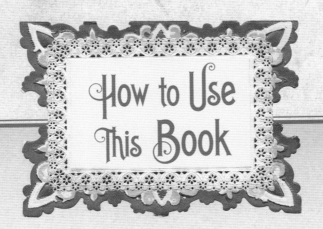

How to Use This Book

General Instructions:

These images are printed on one side only, making it easy to simply cut out the desired image. However, you'll probably want to use them again, so we have included a CD-ROM which contains all of the images individually as well as in the page layout form. The CDs can be used with both PC and Mac formats. Just pop in the disk. On a PC, the file will immediately open to the Home page, which will walk you through how to view and print the images. For Macintosh® users, you will simply double-click on the icon to open. The images may also be incorporated into your computer projects using simple imaging software that you can purchase specifically for this purpose—a perfect choice for digital scrapbooking.

The reference numbers printed on the back of each image in the book are the same ones used on the CD, which will allow you to easily find the image you are looking for. The numbering consists of the book abbreviation, the page number, the image number, and the file format. The first file number (located next to the page number) is for the entire page. For example, BB01-001.jpg would be the entire image for page 1 of *Lace*. These are provided for you on the CD. The second file number is for the top-right image. The numbers continue in a counterclockwise spiral fashion.

Once you have resized your images, added text, created a scrapbook page, etc., you are ready to print them out. Printing on cream or white cardstock, particularly a textured variety, creates a more authentic look. You won't be able to tell that it's a reproduction! If you don't have access to a computer or printer, that's ok. Most photocopy centers can resize and print your images for a nominal fee, or they have do-it-yourself machines that are easy to use.

Ideas for Using the Images:

Scrapbooking: These images are perfect for both heritage and modern scrapbook pages. Simply use the image as a frame, accent piece, or border. For those of you with limited time, the page layouts in this book have been created so that you can use them as they are. Simply print out or photocopy the desired page, attach a photograph into one of the boxes, and you have a beautiful scrapbook page in minutes. For a little dimension, add a ribbon or charm. Be sure to print your images onto acid-free cardstock so the pages will last a lifetime.

Cards: Some computer programs allow images to be inserted into a card template, simplifying cardmaking. If this is not an option, simply use the images as accent pieces on the front or inside of the card. Use a bone folder to score the card's fold to create a more professional look.

Decoupage/Collage Projects: For decoupage or collage projects, photocopy or print the image onto a thinner paper such as copier paper. Thin paper adheres to projects more effectively. Decoupage medium glues and seals the project, creating a gloss or matte finish when dry, thus protecting the image. Vintage images are beautiful when decoupaged to cigar boxes, glass plates, and even wooden plaques. The possibilities are endless.

Fabric Arts: Vintage images can be used in just about any fabric craft imaginable: wall hangings, quilts, bags, or baby bibs. Either transfer the image onto the fabric by using a special iron-on paper, or by printing the image directly onto the fabric, using a temporary iron-on stabilizer that stabilizes the fabric to feed through a printer. These items are available at most craft and sewing stores. If the item will be washed, it is better to print directly on the fabric. For either method, follow the instructions on the package.

Wood Transfers: It is now possible to "print" images on wood. Use this exciting technique to create vintage plaques, clocks, frames, and more. A simple, inexpensive transfer tool is available at most large craft or home improvement stores, or online from various manufacturers. You simply place the photocopy of the image you want, face down, onto the surface and use the tool to transfer the image onto the wood. This process requires a copy from a laser printer, which means you will probably have to get your copies made at a copy center. Refer to manufacturer's instructions for additional details. There are other transfer products available that can be used with wood. Choose the one that is easiest for you.

A Token of True Love

Gallery of Ideas

These *Lace* images can be used in a variety of projects: cards, scrapbook pages, and decoupage projects to name a few. The images can be used as they are shown in the layout, or you can copy and clip out individual images, or even portions or multitudes of images. The following pages contain a collection of ideas to inspire you to use your imagination and create one-of-a-kind treasures.

original page

Many of the designs in this book invite you to replace portions of the original image with personalized photographs, sentiments, and journaling. The cheerful violet borders of this page make wonderful frames for photos of a sunny summer day at the park.

Day at the Park

Day at the Park!

Delightful oval and heart shapes serve as perfect picture frames for the happy couple on this wedding scrapbook page.

original page

Our Wedding Day

Wedding Day

Valentine Memories

So many memories, so little time! To use your Memories of a Lifetime layouts as instant scrapbook pages simply insert your own photographs into the "frames" that are part of each vintage valentine. If you choose you can keep one frame blank to add your own copy or valentine message.

original page

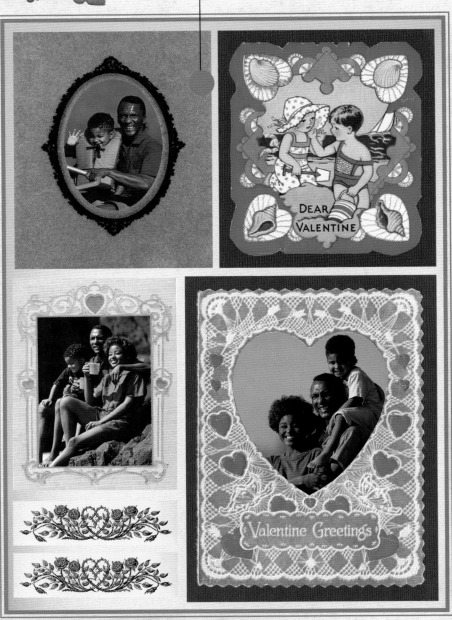

Embellished Journals

For a unique, pretty gift, decoupage layered motifs and patterns onto a playing card and adhere to a blank journal. Embellish with a wisp of lace.

Rectangular images and frames lined with
ribbon create a tidy look for a scrapbook page.
Victorian illustrations, lacy frames, and soft
shades of pink and green add a delicate flair.

Period images and vintage floral motifs are a perfect complement to black-and-white photos from days gone by. Be creative with lace to add drama to a page. Here, lace trim is draped across the corners.

Heritage
Scrapbook Page

Modern Scrapbook Page

Use fancy motifs sparingly for a clean, modern look. This page starts out bold and simple, with modest ribbon and monochromatic tones. An Art Nouveau border and pretty doilies add ornamentation without overwhelming the page.

Vintage Greeting Cards

These fancy-looking greeting cards are easy
to create. Simply adhere vintage illustrations
to a plain card. Cut a length of lace trim and
adhere a portion along the card edge, then tie
the remaining trim in a knot.

Embellished Notebook

A simple notebook becomes a diary for your biggest dreams and ideas with a little embellishing. Decoupage a pretty background and vintage images onto the cover, then add game tiles and a length of lace tied in a bow.

LA01-004   LA01-003   LA01-002

LA01-007

LA01-005

LA01-006

Birthday Greetings

I love you

To My VALENTINE

LA02-003

LA02-002

LA02-004

LA02-007

LA02-005

LA02-006

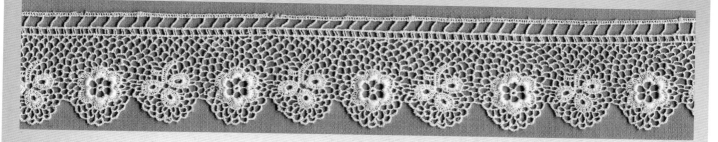

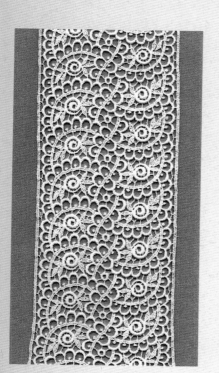

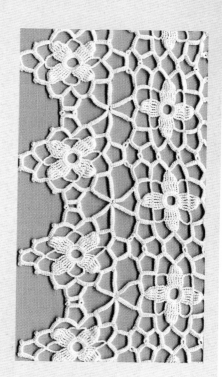

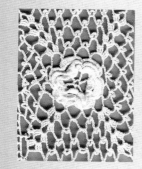

LA03-002

LA03-003   LA03-009   LA03-008

LA03-007

LA03-004

LA03-005   LA03-006

03 — LA03-001

FIGURE NO. 16 CC.

Spanish flounce. In the full b
by a tuck-shirring made at yok
the fronts droop in blouse fas
worn at the neck, long puffs fal
the elbows, and lace flows ove
ribbon being arranged above it
side. Two frills of lace are di
fronts in a festoon. From a s
bon belt falls a long strip of ri
side of it; the jabot is finishe
flounce, and a bow is placed
The costume owes much of its
may be developed in crépon or

White chiffon was used in th
shown at figure No. 7 CC. The
skirt hangs in graceful folds. '
ion at the center, and the fulnes
low ribbon that is knotted at th
and moderately low and is trim
the elbow puff sleeves are deco
ruching. A ribbon rosette is pl
over the upper end of the upri
end of this ribbon are formed tw
be effectively used in making t
is presented in pattern No. 7482

A *chic gown* for a lady is illu

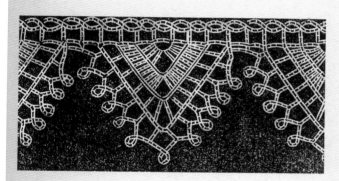

THE DELINEATOR.   97

FASHIONABLE DRESS GOODS.

strangely at variance
t their vogue is very
ound expression last
, which were offered
rjoyed only a limited
ed chiffon followed,
ly in the Autumn;

arranged in some floral or geometrical
device.
From chiffon to lady's-cloth is a consid-
erable stride, yet embroidered or unfinished
perforations contribute their share of at-
tractiveness to the heavy, smooth fabric as
well as to the half-transparent one; and the
fancy is carried out in velveteen with equal
success. Occasionally an entire gown is
evolved from perforated cloth or velveteen,
but more often the eyeletted material is
used only for a portion of a costume, and
in every case it affords an excuse for the
introduction of an enlivening color under-
neath, which sifts through the openings like
sunlight through a lattice of boughs. In
heavy goods, such as cloth or velveteen
(now known also as veloutina), the perforations are either left unfinished or else are
wrought with silk; but in chiffon, taffeta,
Liberty satin and other light-weight fabrics
they are invariably worked, the effect re-
calling the very open "pierced" needlework of a generation ago.
The charm of these novel materials when
made up is admirably exemplified in a
lately devised visiting toilette, in which
perforated cloth in a golden tone of brown
and underlaid with vivid red cashmere is
associated with plain cloth and velvet in
the same shade of brown. The skirt is
composed of four gores, and the rather

FIGURE NO. 3.—BORDER DESIGN.

LA04-003

LA04-002

LA04-008

LA04-007

LA04-004

LA04-006

LA04-005

04 — LA04-001

TO MY VALENTINE

I'm a robber bold,
But not for gold —
I'm after a Valentine;
My quest I'll end,
My little friend —
If you'll say you'll
be mine.

Lo! at thy
Feet I lie —
I am all
thine.
One smile do
not deny
Thy Valentine.

LA05-003   LA05-002

LA05-004   LA05-005

LA05-001

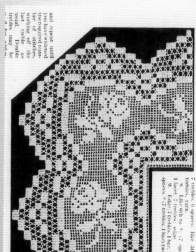

LA06-004

LA06-003

LA06-002

LA06-005

LA06-011

LA06-010

LA06-006   LA06-007

LA06-008

LA06-009

LA06-001

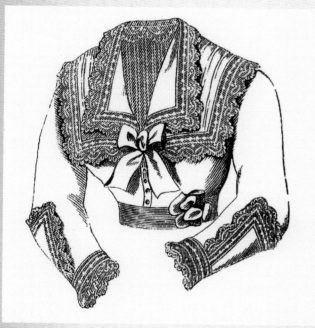

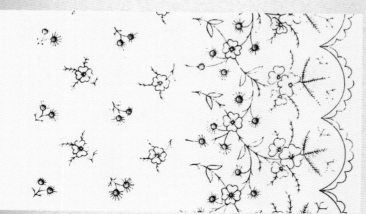

EVERY-DAY DRESSES, GARMENTS, Etc.

BY EMILY H. MAY.

No. 1—Is a walking-dress, of either zephyr, gingham, or sateen. The underskirt is in wide kilt-plaits all around. The over-drapery forms a long point in front, the back in irregular loops. The material is fulled into the shoulder, opening over a V-shaped front of velvet or surah; cuffs and collar to match. Loops of narrow velvet or gros-grain ribbon trim the skirt on left side. Hat of straw, veiled in dotted lace and trimmed with butterfly bows of velvet or gros-grain ribbon to match the gown. Parasol of the same material as the dress. Fourteen to fifteen yards of material will be required.

No. 2—Is an embroidered nainsook dress. The foundation of plain nainsook has a narrow plaited ruffle on the edge. Over this, a deep flounce of the embroidery is kilt-plaited. The

No. 1.

No. 2.

LA07-003

LA07-002

LA07-004

LA07-007

LA07-005

LA07-006

LA07-001

GOOD LUCK

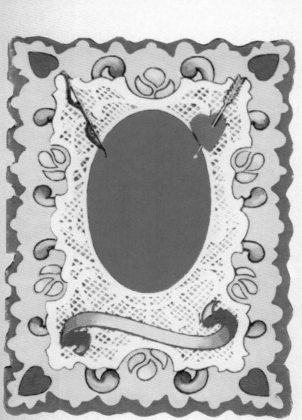

PETERSON'S MAGAZINE—MARCH, 1888

LA08-003

LA08-004   LA08-002

LA08-005   LA08-006

LA08-001

LA09-002

A Token of True Love

476 THE DELINEATOR.

ARTISTIC NEEDLEWORK.

(For Illustrations see Pages 476 to 478.)

FIGURES NOS. 1, 2 AND 3.—DESIGN FOR HONITON LACE.—This pattern was especially designed for the ladies' bodice decoration, pattern No. 7866, which costs 5d. or 10 cents, and is shown with the lace applied at figure No. 53 Y on page 461. The design is here given in actual size and may be easily traced by joining the sections as marked by the letters A, B, C and D. A portion of the design fully worked is shown at figure No. 1, the material being cut from beneath the fancy stitches. The remainder of this section and those shown at figures Nos. 2 and 3 should be similarly worked, only the method of applying the lace braid being pictured. "Modern Lace Making," published by us at 2s. or 50 cents, contains full instructions for the work.

FIGURE NO. 4.—FANCY SCREEN.—Bamboo provides a pretty frame-work for this screen, the center of which is dull-green grosgrain silk elaborately embroidered with gold and silver cord and spangles.

FIGURE NO. 5.—PIN-CUSHION.—Odd and pretty is the pin-cushion here pictured. It is of hexagonal shape, the sides being of dark brocaded satin. The top is formed of alternate sections of plain, delicate blue and silver brocaded satin; these sections are separated by silk cords made into loops at the ends and at the center. Such a cushion affords ample opportunity for striking color combinations.

CHILDREN'S CORNER.

(For Illustrations see Pages 478 and 479.)

Cheerfully you give up your games to go nutting, for the nuts are now ripe and ready to fall and Jack Frost has not yet come to nip fingers and noses. The nuts which you gather taste far sweeter than those you buy, so hasten away, little lads and lasses, and fill your baskets to overflowing. How shall

FIGURE NO. 1.—SECTION OF DESIGN FOR HONITON LACE.—(For Description see "Artistic Needlework," on this page.)

you crack the nuts after they are gathered? If a metal nut-cracker is not at hand, you may use a stone, which, after all, does it work well enough when out of doors; but you will reserve some of the nuts for eating by the glowing nursery fire, into which you will throw the shells. Don't they crackle and burn brightly, these nut shells? But neither nurse nor mamma will permit the use of the primitive stone nut-cracker in the nursery. So I will tell you how to make one that will work as successfully as any for which the government has granted a patent.

Two oblong pieces of rather stout board form the sides of the nut-cracker pictured at figure No. 1. Cut a deep notch in one end of each side, sawing the other end off square. Make three holes in each square end and fasten the two sides together with wire hooks, as shown in the picture. The cracker is

LA10-003

LA10-002

LA10-006

LA10-004

LA10-005

LA10-001

made up in a combination of figured French ... with a decoration of velvet ribbon and ... sides and may be gathered or plaited bands of velvet ribbon falling low over ...

MODERN LACE-MAKING.

The designs presented in this department for the current month are all very popular and convey a partial idea of the variety of that can be made of darned net. A scarf or kerchief of rosebuds made like those of this design would be

FIGURE No. 1.—DARNED-NET EDGING, WITH OVER-WROUGHT STITCH. (FULL SIZE.)

FIGURE No. 2.—BOW-KNOT DESIGN FOR MODERN LACE.

signs that may also be found in our book upon "The Art of Modern Lace-Making."

The designs seen at figures Nos. 2 and 4 may be made as wide or narrow as desired, or of white or écru braid, according to the fabric it is to be used with.

DARNED-NET EDGING, WITH OVER-WROUGHT STITCH.

FIGURE No. 1.—This handsome edging is darned on a wide strip of net with coarse and fine embroidery cotton, and after the pattern is completed the lower edge of the net is cut away. The coarse cotton is used to outline the design and fill in some of the central portions, while the fine is darned in between the outer and center portions, and is used for the over-wrought portions. These portions are "run" back and forth loosely to form a raised foundation for the ... and rose-centers before the over-wrought

The full sleeves are completed with ... decorated with embroidered edging. ... in the stylish five-gored skirt, which is ... front and sides and may be gathered or p ...

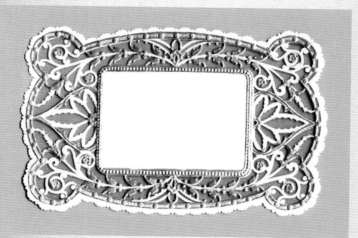

LA11-004   LA11-003   LA11-002

LA11-005

LA11-008

LA11-006   LA11-007

LA11-001

Square for Inset, Chelsea Pattern

Napkin-Corner, Rose-Design

Napkin-Corner, Vintage-Pattern

Corner for Lunchcloth, Vintage-Pattern

LA12-003   LA12-002

LA12-004

                                                  LA12-007

LA12-005   LA12-006

LA12-001

DEAR
VALENTINE

Valentine Greetings

LA13-003

LA13-002

LA13-004

LA13-006

LA13-005

LA13-001

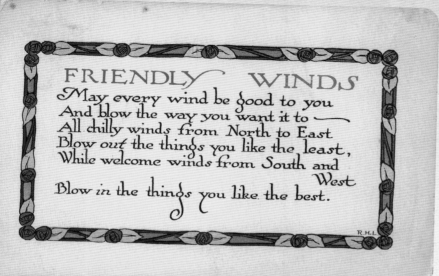

FRIENDLY WINDS

May every wind be good to you
And blow the way you want it to —
All chilly winds from North to East
Blow out the things you like the least,
While welcome winds from South and West
Blow in the things you like the best.

R.H.L.

DESIGN NO. 81.

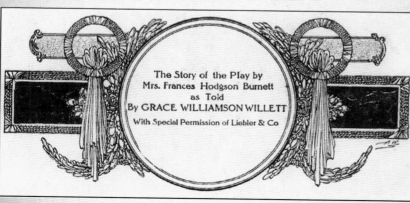

The Story of the Play by Mrs. Frances Hodgson Burnett as Told By GRACE WILLIAMSON WILLETT With Special Permission of Liebler & Co

LA14-003

LA14-002

LA14-007

LA14-006

LA14-004

LA14-005

14 LA14-001

DESCRIPTION OF BRIDAL ATTIRE SHOWN ON OPPOSITE PAGE.

For "the fairest festival of life" the demands of the toilette are not arbitrary, but the bride will always seek to impart to her toilette a certain dignity and grace. A rich faille princesse with satin brocaded figures and *moiré antique façons* are the newest fabrics for Autumn bridal gowns. Equally handsome and just as popular, however, are white corded silk, white satin, rich *peau de soie*, satin duchesse, etc., enriched with pearl passementerie, lace and orange blossoms. Inexpensive and unassuming is a bridal toilette of brocaded taffeta silk, yet it is tasteful and pretty and can be made to do duty afterwards at receptions and dressy functions. Simplicity should characterize the toilette of the youthful bride. The various degrees of elegance in bridal toilettes is largely determined by the circle of friends the bride is to gather about her. For a small home wedding, a travelling gown is sometimes worn, if the bride is to depart soon after the ceremony. Youthful brides who wear a toilette of white silk generally add a tulle veil that falls like a cloud about the figure.

FIGURE D52.—PAGE'S COSTUME.—This illustrates a Boys' costume. The pattern, which is No. 749 and costs 1s. 3d. or 30 cents, is in seven sizes for boys from four to sixteen years old, and is shown again

gles ornament the elbow puff sleeves, which are banded with the spangled trimming at the elbow. A ribbon belt encircles the waist.

The seven-gored skirt is smooth fitting at the front and sides and may be gathered or plaited at the back. It is trimmed with lace jabots at the side-front seams and powdered with grouped spangles to correspond with the sleeves.

The color should be selected with due thought to its suitability to the blonde or brunette complexion for which it is intended.

FIGURE D54.—BRIDE'S TOILETTE.—This illustrates a Ladies' basque-waist and trained skirt. The basque-waist pattern, which is No. 8671 and costs 1s. 3d. or 30 cents, is in thirteen sizes for ladies from twenty-eight to forty-six inches, bust measure, and is differently portrayed on page 441. The skirt pattern, which is No. 8557 and costs 1s. 3d. or 40 cents, is in nine sizes for ladies from twenty to thirty-six inches, waist measure, and

8671   8671

FIGURE No. 7.

FIGURE No. 8.
FIGURES NOS. 6, 7 AND 8.—
LADIES' DUTCH BONNETS.

FIGURE No.

HAT.

FIGURES

FIGURE No. 9.—LITTLE GIRLS' BONNET.—
(Cut by Pattern No. 7585; 5 sizes; Ages,
1 to 9 years; price 5d. or 10 cents.

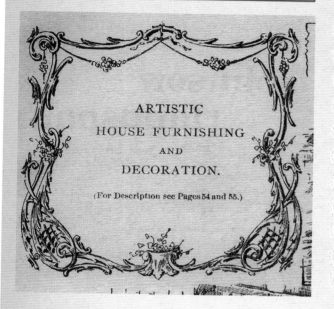

ARTISTIC

HOUSE FURNISHING

AND

DECORATION.

(For Description see Pages 54 and 55.)

Illustrations

8367

LA15-004

LA15-003

LA15-002

LA15-005

LA15-001

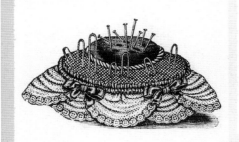

LA16-004   LA16-003   LA16-002

LA16-005   LA16-012   LA16-011

LA16-006   LA16-010

LA16-007   LA16-008   LA16-009

LA16-001

LA17-004   LA17-003   LA17-002

LA17-005   LA17-0010   LA17-009

LA17-006   LA17-011   LA17-008

LA17-007

LA17-001

LA18-002

LA18-003

LA18-001

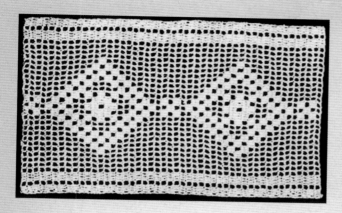

ending with 9. 1 space. 7 trebles. 3 spaces. 4 trebles. 1 space. 4 trebles. 4 spaces; edge.

for
like
h 6
miss
w).
n 2
nue
4
odd
gin
ere
nue
n 4
nue
t

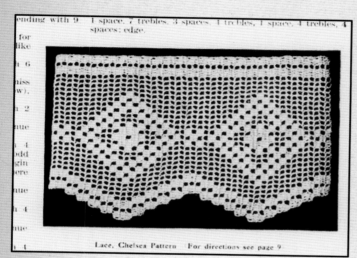

Lace, Chelsea Pattern   For directions see page 9

36.   Four spaces, 4 trebles, and continue like 52d row
Continued on page 9

row.

e, turn.
spaces; edge.
space. 4 trebles. 3

edge.
ce) twice, turn.

is com-
half the
l.
bles to
nts 1st
g trebles
nd 1 at
of treble
ow, slip-
n row, or

urn.
n treble
, slip to

hain. 2.
ow back.

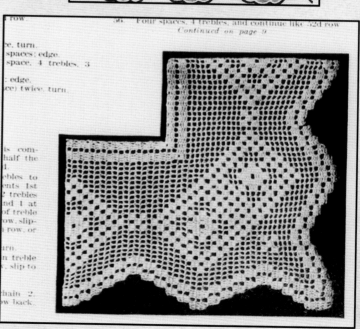

LA19-002

LA19-003

LA19-007

LA19-004

LA19-005   LA19-006

LA19-001

To my
Valentine

LA20-003

LA20-002

LA20-004

LA20-005

LA20-006

LA20-001

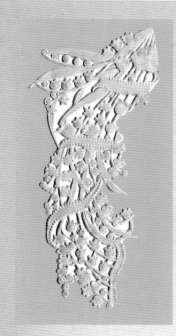

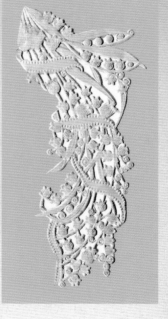

LA21-004

LA21-003

LA21-002

LA21-008

LA21-005

LA21-006

LA21-007

— LA21-001

Venetian Iron Work.

PART XI.

BY J. HARRY ADAMS.

The illustrations given this month not only afford many practical and artistic suggestions for the ambitious amateur, but also serve to convey a good idea of the general adaptability of bent iron work. The designs heretofore presented have been more or less classified, so that, while several patterns for the same kind of object were always

above the desk or table; but if the receiv... without feet, the bottom may be covered wi... fastened to the wood with glue. The e...

DESIGN No. 77.

DESIGN No. 78.

provided, the number of different classes represented was comparatively small, including principally screens, candlesticks, hanging sconces, fairy-lamps, candle-brackets, match-boxes, burnt-match receivers, jardinières, picture-frames, easels, lamps and lanterns. In this and the next paper, however, will be found a collection of miscellaneous designs, each of which will doubtless bring to mind a group of similar objects that can be developed with equal success in the thin iron strips bound strongly together with bands or wires.

Both useful and ornamental is the little paper-and-envelope rack pictured at design No. 77, which may be utilized for stationery upon a writing desk, or else as a receptacle for photographs or cards upon a table. The bottom should be a piece of wood measuring from a quarter to three-eighths of an inch in thickness and about six inches in length; the width may be varied according to the use for which the receptacle is intended. For an envelope rack three inches will be a good width, while a photograph-rack may measure from four to five inches wide. Three uprights must be made of light iron scroll-work after the pattern illustrated; in this case the strips of metal are not more than an eighth of an inch in width, but if a larger rack than the one described were desired, strips somewhat wider in proportion should be used. The same design must be followed for the two outer uprights, but the middle one may be formed

LA22-003　　　　　　　　　　　　　LA22-002

LA22-004　　　　　　　　　　　　　LA22-006

LA22-005

22 — LA22-001

LA23-003

LA23-002

LA23-008

LA23-004

LA23-007

LA23-005

LA23-006

LA23-001

LA24-004　　　　　　　LA24-003　　　　　　LA24-002

LA24-009

LA24-005

LA24-006

LA24-007　　　　　　　LA24-008

24 — BB24-001

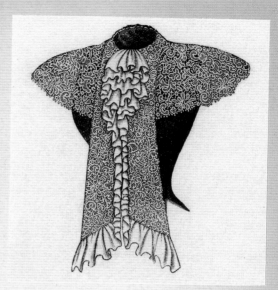

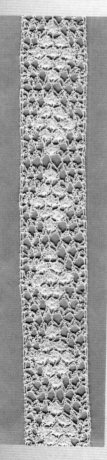

LA25-003   LA25-002

LA25-004   LA25-009   LA25-008

LA25-010

LA25-005   LA25-006   LA25-007

A Message of Love

To the One I love.

Health and peace

D. 41.   D. 42.

LA26-003

LA26-004

LA26-002

LA26-005

LA26-009

LA26-006

LA26-008

LA26-007

LA26-001

LA27-004   LA27-003   LA27-002

LA27-010   LA27-009   LA27-008

LA27-005   LA27-006   LA27-007

27 — LA27-001

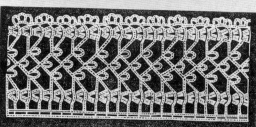

LA28-002

LA28-003   LA28-008   LA28-007

LA28-009

LA28-004   LA28-010   LA28-006

LA28-005

LA28-001

STYLISH LINGERIE.

(For Illustrations see Page 401.)

Waist decorations still hold general favor, the conservative woman realizing how important is their function in a limited wardrobe. These fashionable accessories when judiciously selected can make one plain gown do service for several occasions requiring dressy attire and at the same time lend a touch of daintiness that would be difficult to attain by any other means. Silk, satin, velvet, lace and all diaphanous

1177

LADIES' CLOSED UMBRELLA DRAWERS.

(For Description see Page 446.)

fabrics enter into their construction and added trimmings, consisting of lace edging, insertion, gimps and passementeries, are frequently seen.

FIGURES NOS. 53 Y AND 54 Y.—LADIES' HIGH AND LOW NECKED GARNITURES.—The low-necked garniture is portrayed at figure No. 53 Y made of white silk. It is pointed at the back and over the shoulders and at the center of the front is extended to reach to the waist-line. A frill of lace edging follows all the edges of the garniture, that at the neck edge falling over it without fulness. Other ornamentation is supplied by pearl trimming.

In the high-necked garniture, shown at figure No. 54 Y, plum-colored silk is portrayed. A standing collar completes the neck and below it, in circular yoke outline, are applied three rows of white lace insertion. White lace edging trims the loose edges

decoration, black Astrakhan f... A neat completion is furnishe... FIGURE NO. 57 Y.—LADIES' ... addition to a partially worn b... silk was chosen for the garnit... standing collar, which are of... lace. A bow of ribbon is pl... frills of white lace complete th... is included in pattern No. 2...

FIGURES NOS. 58 Y AND 59 ... —At figure No. 58 Y is displ... low, round outline at the top... edge. White satin was selecte... outlining its lower edge.

The decoration pictured at... same pattern, No. 1174, wh... garniture is pictured worn c... costs 1s. 3d. or 30 cents. ... advantage developed in crea... green and a dark-green silk s... is ornamented by bows of t... to the stock. The waist de...

BOLERO COSTUME, HAVING A ... -PIECE SKIRT GATHERED AT ...CK. (TO BE MADE WITH OR WITH-... THE PEPLUM AND ÉPAULETTES.)

(For Illustrations see this Page.)

...1.—At figure D 41 in this maga-...ostume is differently portrayed. ...tume is here shown in a combination ...amel's-hair and silk and yellow lace ...The waist has a smooth back with-...at the center and is closely fitted ...ust darts and under-arm and side-...s. A double jabot of lace edging ... front edge of the right front nearly ...ist-line and its ends are carried in ... the joining of the standing collar ... the shoulders. A wide wrinkled ...sses the front and is included in ...arm seam at the right side and

joined in ... and sepa... flares sty... four yard... the med... fectly sn... taken up... skirt is ... skirt spe... back. ... center se...

The ne... in such w... and Scot... ively in t... and lace ...

We ha... for ladie... inches, b... size, the...

8631

LA29-003

LA29-002

LA29-004

LA29-005

LA29-006

LA29-007

LA29-001

House Furnishing and Decoration.

A pretext is found in these comfort-loving days for establishing a cosey corner even in the library. Heretofore the furnishing of this apartment was characterized by a severity almost uninviting. Happily, other ideas now prevail in furnishing, and the homemaker's opportunity for introducing original effects has been extended. A tastefully appointed library corner is shown in the first illustration. An oriental rug lies upon the polished wood floor and a figured paper in pretty half-tones covers the wall. A grate fire sends its cheerful glow out into the apartment and glints upon the brass fender, casting shadows across the tiled hearth and facings. Upon the mantel are vases and above are pictures and a marble bust. Book shelves with cabinets are built into the wall between the mantel and window and beneath the latter is an upholstered settee, also made stationary, the whole forming an inviting corner. The window is hung with a simple drapery of white muslin. By night the apartment is lighted by a wrought-iron standard lamp, the light coming through a green silk shade and falling upon the settee next which it is stationed.

A glimpse of a boudoir is shown in the second engraving. A fancy-bordered rug of dark-red velvet filling is spread over a floor covered with matting—its Summer dress. A large dressing-case of birch with bevelled mirror stands at one end and above it hangs a prettily-framed landscape in water colors. In the bay window is built a settee upholstered with light-blue denim and rendered additionally comfortable by pillows. The window has white Swiss sash curtains held back with ribbons. Portières of dark-blue denim are adjusted at the entrance of the bay and above it on a shelf are old-fashioned platters and jugs. An upholstered chair completes the appointment of this delightful retreat.

The Colonial dining-room pictured in the third engraving carries one in fancy back to Revolutionary days. Upon the oak floor is a large rug and paper in a small blue-and-white figure covers the walls. The mantel of white-enamelled wood is built above a fire-place with iron andirons upon which the hickory logs may be piled high. The arched window next the mantel has long sash curtains and a half sash curtain of white Swiss in addition to a white shade. Below the grille in the door-ways hang portières of figured white-and-blue velours, and between the door-ways stands a heavy oak sideboard with its square-paned crystal closet. A table spread with a bordered blue velours cloth supporting a growing palm and leather covered chairs complete the furnishings.

LA30-003

LA30-002

LA30-007

LA30-004

LA30-008

LA30-005

LA30-006

LA30-001

LA31-003

LA31-002

LA31-004

LA31-005

LA31-001

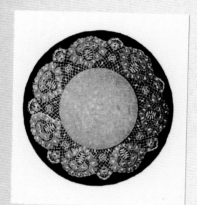

LA32-002

LA32-003   LA32-006

LA32-004   LA32-005

LA32-001

Birthday
Greetings

LA33-003

LA33-002

LA33-004

LA33-005

LA33-006

LA33-001

Trust in
the Lord.

Psa. XXXVII: 3.

LA34-003   LA34-002

LA34-004   LA34-005

LA34-001

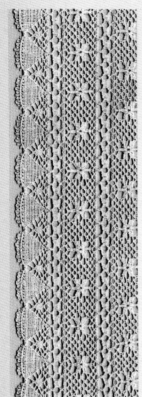

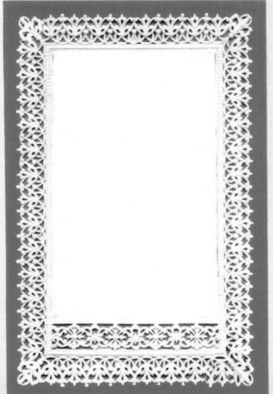

LA35-002

LA35-003   LA35-008   LA35-007

LA35-004   LA35-005   LA35-006

LA35-001

LA36-003

LA36-002

LA36-006

LA36-004

LA36-005

LA36-001

BY EMMA HAYWOOD.

(MRS. HAYWOOD WILL WILLINGLY FURNISH ANY FURTHER INFORMATION OR DESIGNS DESIRED. LETTERS TO HER MAY BE ADDRESSED CARE OF THE EDITOR OF THE DELINEATOR.)

In the third paper of this series designs were given for a burse, chalice veil and Eucharistic stole. These are in general use on every altar of the Episcopal church at the celebration of the Holy Eucharist, but it is a lamentable fact that—though to this extent a decent ordering of things is observed, yet in the majority of the same churches the priest himself is not properly vested. Why is this? In some cases it is, perhaps, because he does not appreciate the value of a ritual that is intended to reflect the worship in heaven as shown by the Apostle St. John in his vision of the adoring hosts of Heaven engaged in solemn service, but far oftener he neglects these adjuncts to a reverential worship, because he is unable to combat the prejudices of his congregation. Such prejudice is born of ignorance or, worse still, of wilful misconception. It formed no part of the Reformation that separated the Anglican church from Rome. This unreasoning prejudice is fast dying out, just as the spirit of antagonism to vested choirs and altar lights has died.

The sacred vestments required by the rubrics for the girdle. The chasuble is an oval garment with an aperture for the head to pass through and is partly open at the sides for the free use of the hands. It is the peculiar vestment of the priest, worn by him only at the celebration of the Holy Communion, and it is usually spoken of as The Vestment. It is emblematic of the royal robe put on our Lord in mockery by the soldiers, just as the maniple and girdle are to remind us of the cords with which he was bound.

The entire set of silk vestments may be embroidered as richly as possible. When true and opportunity serve, the work cannot be too fine or too elaborate, while the material for the vestments should be of the richest brocade lined with good, soft silk. This is, of course, very costly; so, when it cannot be afforded, plain satin or ribbed silk may be substituted. Indeed, in very poor parishes the vestments are sometimes made of pure linen embroidered with flax thread. Linen vestments do not need any lining. Their appearance is really and far preferable to omitting the use of them altogether. Colored linens are now brought to great...

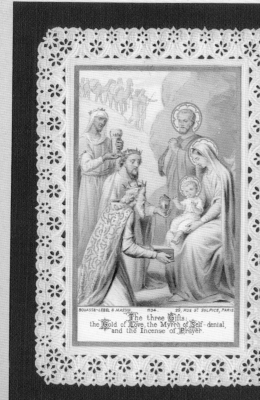

LA37-003

LA37-002

LA37-004

LA37-007

LA37-005

LA37-006

LA37-001

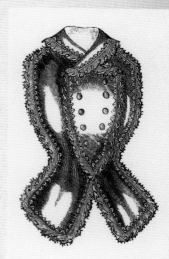

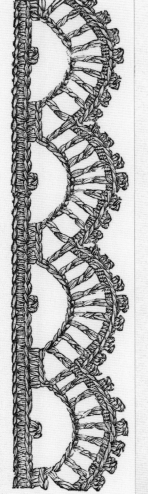

a b c d e f g
h i j k l m n
o p q r s t
u v w x y z

LA38-003   LA38-002

LA38-004   LA38-007

LA38-005   LA38-006

LA38-001

LA39-002

LA40-003 LA40-002

LA40-004 LA40-005

LA40-001

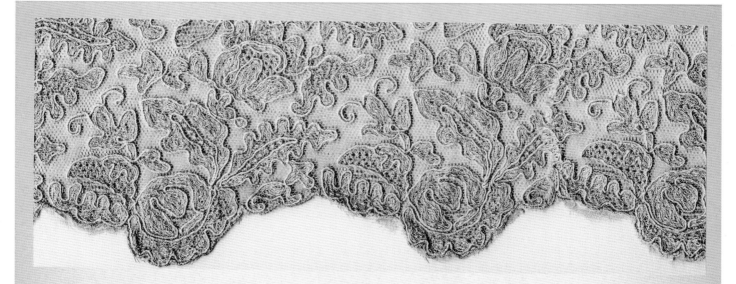

character to an otherwise simple basque.

Tapering box-plaits applied to a French basque-waist are certain to give the wearer a becomingly slender appearance.

The chemisette is still fashionable with double-breasted basques that fall below the hips.

The sleeve puffs of a very fluffy waist are arranged

. 202 L.

203 L.—
LARS.—
rate the
. 7359
10 cents.
o 28.)

umference at the bottom.
irt is the introduction of

r amplitude in the skirt
year ago; otherwise the

FIGURE NO. 203 L.

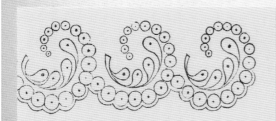

LA41-002

LA41-003   LA41-009   LA41-008

                            LA41-009   LA41-007

        LA41-004   LA41-005   LA41-006

FIGURE NO. 3.—SQUARE IN MODERN POINT LACE.

essary to definitely describe them. bstituted for those here illustrated. a scarf end in connection with the in the September DELINEATOR for

1891, if the braid selected is sufficiently fine. When coarser braid is chosen, the square will be pretty for doilies, tidies or the center of a table spread. The design may be daintily made up of ribbon, with silk for the stitches. In this event it may be set into a scarf or drapery of China or Surah silk with charming results.

DESIGN FOR TABLE SCARF IN BATTENBURG LACE.

FIGURE NO. 4.—The scarf end

LA42-004   LA42-003   LA42-002

LA42-005

LA42-006

LA42-001

LA43-002

LA43-003

LA43-004

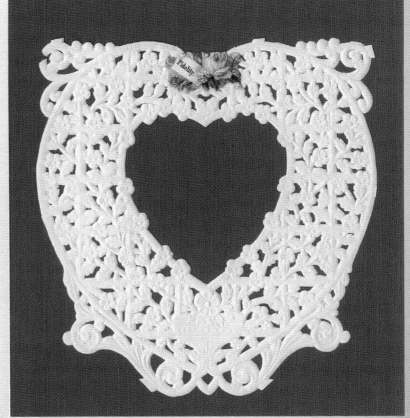

LA44-003

LA44-002

LA44-006

LA44-004

LA44-005

LA45-002

Ladies' Costume, Consisting of a Norfolk Basque with Plain Laid On and a Seven-Gored Skirt Side-Plaited at the Back (Copyright): 13 sizes. Bust measure, 28 to 46 inches. Any size, 1s. 3d. or 40 cents.

Ladies' Costume, with Ripple Peplum and a Seven-Gored Skirt Box-Plaits at the Back (Copyright). Bust meas., 28 to 46 ins. Any size, 1s.

Ladies' Costume (Closed at the Left Side, with Princess Back (To be Made with a High-or Round Neck and with Full-Length or Elbow Puff Sleeves) (Copyright): 13 sizes. Bust measure, 28 to 46 inches. Any size, 1s. 3d. or 30 cents.

Ladies' Costume having a Six-Gored Skirt with a Straight Back-Breadth (To be Made With or Without the Fichu and with Full-Length or Elbow Double Puff Sleeves) (Copyr'G): 13 sizes. Bust meas., 28 to 46 ins. Any size, 1s. 3d. or 40 cts.

Ladies' Costume, with Ripple Peplum and a Seven-Gored Skirt Side-Plaited at the Back. (In Louis XV. Style) (Copyright): 13 sizes. Bust measure, 28 to 46 ins. Any size, 1s.

Ladies' Costume, having a Bolero (That may be Omitted) and a Three-Piece Skirt Gathered at the Back (To be Made with Full-Length or Elbow Puff Sleeves) (Copyright): 13 sizes. Bust measure, 28 to 46 inches. Any size, 1s. rd. or 40 cents.

Ladies' Costume, with Five-Gored Skirt Gathered at the Back (Copyright). 13 sizes. Bust measure, 28 to 46 Any size, 1s. 3d. or 40 cents.

shoulder. It forms two long points over each sleeve, two points at the back and a point at each side of a graduated strap extension at the center of the front. The strap extension is caught at the waist-line and droops prettily, and the decoration is outlined with lace insertion and edging. When the decoration is made high-necked, it is finished with a standing collar about which a ribbon stock is usually adjusted.

Silk in any of the pretty varieties now sold, as well as lawn and other sheer fabrics, will be selected for this decoration and trimmed with pearl bead gimp or lace.

We have pattern No. 1182 in three sizes, small, medium and large. In the medium size, the waist decoration requires one yard of goods twenty-two inches wide, or seven-eighths of a yard

1183

1182

Ladies' Waist Decoration. (To be Made High or Low Necked.)

thirty-six or more inches wide. Price of pattern, 3d. or 5 cents.

LADIES' FRILL AND PUFF. (EITHER ONE TO BE ADDED TO CORSET-COVERS OR JOINED TO THE ARMS'-EYES OF BLOUSES, SHIRT-WAISTS, ETC., TO HOLD THE SLEEVES OUT AT THE TOP.)

1171 **1171**

LADIES' FRILL AND PUFF. (EITHER ONE TO BE ADDED TO CORSET-COVERS OR JOINED TO THE ARMS'-EYES OF BLOUSES, SHIRT-WAISTS, ETC., TO HOLD THE SLEEVES OUT AT THE TOP.)

at the top. Both are highly popular and perform their office equally well, hence the choice of either is a matter of personal taste. They may be sewed to the arms'-eyes of the waist or added to the corset-cover, as preferred. They are here shown made of cambric. The puff is gathered at the top and bottom and finished with a narrow band that fits the arm comfortably. A frill of lace edging drooping from the lower edge of the band makes the puff decorative. The frill is shallower than the puff and is deepened at the shoulder; it is gathered at its upper edge and is decorated at its lower edge with a row of lace edging.

Lawn, cambric, nainsook and various thin materials are chosen for the frill and puff and embroidered or lace edging will generally be used to give a dainty finish.

We have pattern No. 1171 in three sizes, small, medium and large. In the medium size, the two frills require half a

rich cardinal shade, by pattern No. 8647, price 10d. or 20 cents. The skirt is full and falls from a square yoke, the skirt being smocked at the top in several straight rows above a series of points, red silk being used for the stitching. A line of fancy stitching also runs along the top of the hem finishing the of the skirt. Over the yoke falls a pointed collar d with fancy stitching. The full sleeves are smocked wrists to simulate cuffs, and below the smocking th falls in a frill over the little hand. An edging Valenciennes lace is se inside the frill and con a very dainty effect. who has very good tast herself best in this gown

A number of apron made of white cambri nainsook, dimity and lawn, two styles being pr

One has a full skirt with a hemstitched hem, a yoke in a V at the top, which may be cut from deep embroider ing, and short, full sleeves that may also be made of edging ends are bowed over the backs. tern No. 8513, price 10d. or 20 vided in pattern No. 8604, cents. price 7d. or 15 cents. It is shirred twice at the top far enough The other style from the edge to form a frill heading. The sides are hollowed out to form arms'-eyes, and ties cross the shoulders and are bowed on top. This is a practical apron for wear over gowns

of the sleeves re followed by everal shirt e cambric and y pattern No. ts. The back the fronts are g applied at orresponding

users of the lded in front t is arranged plait is also de-plaits are ubens collar The pattern or 20 cents. assie of three s is her first l it is not an lainty white ashmere are her morning made with a joined to a

8543

8534

8647 **8647**

8647 **8647**

LA46-004   LA46-003   LA46-002

LA46-005   LA46-008

LA46-006   LA46-007

LA46-001

Styles for Little Folks.

(For Illustration see this Page.)

RE No. 344 T.—LITTLE GIRLS' DRESS.

44 T.—This illustrates a Little Girls' dress. The pat-
o. 4315 and costs 10d. or 20 cents, is in seven sizes
om one-half to six years of age, and is differently
e 128 of this magazine.

l silk in a light and a dark shade of brown are styl-
e dress in the present instance. The full, round skirt
ong and falls in free, graceful folds from gathers at
it joins the body; and the lower edge is decorated
f silk, upon which moderately large cabochons are
ed. The short body has a front and backs, which
e top in Pompadour shape and gathered to produce
ect across the front and at each side of the closing;
lled in with square yoke-portions of silk, the edges
tlined with frills of silk to emphasize the yoke
ge of the yoke is decorated with cabochons, and

are trimmed at the edges with frills of embroide
ornament the edges of the deep collar, which is in
flare widely at the front and back; and frills outl
side edges of patch pockets at the front. The u
pockets are trimmed with insertion, and simila
the side-front seams. Sash-ties included in the
are prettily bowed at the center of the back.

Aprons of this kind are variously developed in cr
percale, lawn, gingham and sheer muslins of vario
of Medici, torchon or Italian lace, white and col
edging, bias bands of the material, feather-stit
able braid, etc., may supply the garniture, beir

FIGURE NO. 344 T.   FIGURE NO. 345 T.

FIGURE No. 344 T.—LITTLE GIRLS' DRESS.—This illustrates Pattern No. 4315 (copyright), price 10d.
or 20 cents. FIGURE No. 345 T.—CHILD'S APRON.—This illustrates Pattern
No. 4316 (copyright), price 10d. or 20 cents.
(For Descriptions see this Page.)

THE DELINEATOR.

347 T.—CHILD'S NIGHT-DRAWERS.

(For Illustration see Page 129.)

—This illustrates a Child's night-drawers. The
4297 and costs
twelve sizes for
twelve years of
ved in two views
agazine.

el was selected
present instance.
s adjusted by in-
eam at the center
, the latter seam
eck of the body.
ly long, and their
d with hems that
. The body por-
ulder and under-
sed at the back
l buttons. The
nd to the waist-
re deepened gra-
here they form
g of the draw-
tion is gathered
and buttons and
he closing. The
ed at the wrists
, and at the neck
d along the top.
on flannel will
able drawers for
slin will be most
eather. Narrow

joined in a short seam at the center of the
forms a pretty framing for the face, a large fr
top, and white ribbon ties are bowed benea
Corded silk, Surah, merino, fancy cloth,
pretty cloaks o
broidery or bra
decoration. T
Bengaline, Mar
or any pretty v
ture, and a ruc
ennes lace may

FIGURES Nos
FANTS' SACKS.—
these two figu
same pattern—
which costs 5d.
size, and both s
trated on page
The sack pict
is shown made
trimmed with r
rangement of w
of a single secti
slashed at the
reversed to for
caught together
shape the sleev
which are reve
cuffs. The sack
the collar with
ranged in a dair

FIGURE No. 346 T.—CHILD'S HOUSE TOILETTE.—This consists of Little
Girls' Apron No. 4298 (copyright), price 7d. or 15 cents; and
Dress No. 4168 (copyright), price 10d. or 20 cents.
(For Description see Page 127.)

frills of lace or embroidery may trim the
neck and wrist edges, or any other simple mode of ornamentation may be
adopted.

FIGURES Nos. 348 T, 349 T, 350 T and
351 T.—STYLES FOR INFANTS.

are followed by a plain row of braid,
inside which a row of similar braid
is coiled to produce a fanciful effect.
Cream-white flannel was selected
for the sack displayed at figure No.
350 T. The garment is adjusted by
under-arm gores and a center seam,
and the fronts are closed at the top

Remember me.

LA47-003

LA47-002

LA47-006

LA47-004

LA47-005

LA48-002

LA49-002

LA49-003

LA49-001

LA50-002

LA50-003   LA50-006   LA50-005

LA50-004

LA50-001

LA51-002

LA52-002

LA52-003

LA52-004

LA53-002

LA53-003

LA53-004

LA53-001

LA54-002

Printed by E. Hochdanz, Stuttgart, Germany.

ORNAMENTS ON WOOD AND METALS ETC.

LA55-002

PERSAN

Lith.par Laugier.

Imp.Firmin-Didot fr.Fils & C.ie Paris.

LA56-002

LA57-002

LA57-003

LA57-004